PIANO SOLO

HOW TO TRAIN YOUR DRAGON
THE HIDDEN WORLD

MUSIC FROM THE
MOTION PICTURE SOUNDTRACK
MUSIC BY **JOHN POWELL**

Piano Solo Arrangements by Batu Sener

ISBN: 978-1-5400-4930-8

Visit Hal Leonard Online at
www.halleonard.com

Contact us:
Hal Leonard
7777 West Bluemound Road
Milwaukee, WI 53213
Email: info@halleonard.com

In Europe, contact:
Hal Leonard Europe Limited
42 Wigmore Street
Marylebone, London, W1U 2RN
Email: info@halleonardeurope.com

In Australia, contact:
Hal Leonard Australia Pty. Ltd.
4 Lentara Court
Cheltenham, Victoria, 3192 Australia
Email: info@halleonard.com.au

HOW TO TRAIN YOUR
DRAGON
THE HIDDEN WORLD

LEGEND HAS IT/ CLIFFSIDE PLAYTIME

By JOHN POWELL

TOOTHLESS: SMITTEN.

By JOHN POWELL

EXODUS!

By JOHN POWELL

THIRD DATE

By JOHN POWELL

NEW 'NEW TAIL'

By JOHN POWELL

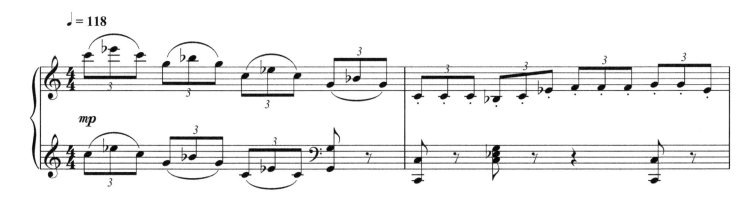

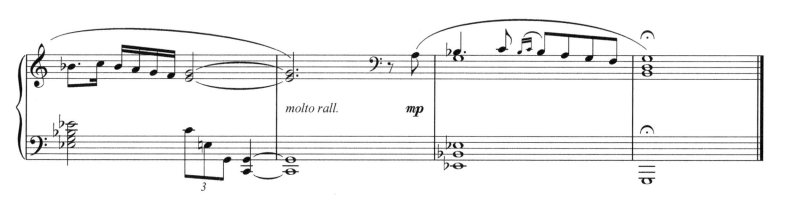

FURIES IN LOVE

By JOHN POWELL

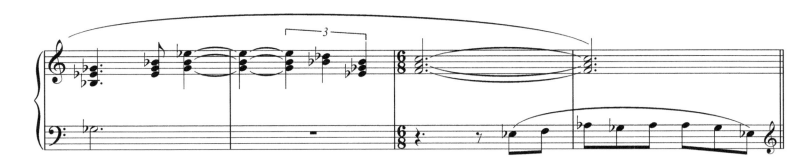

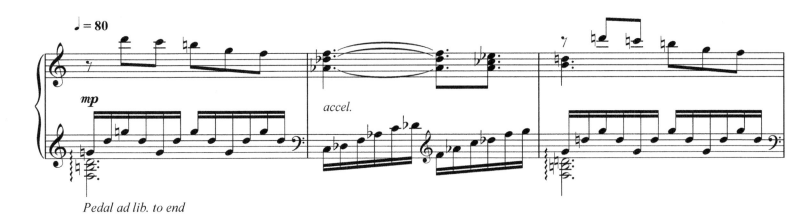

Pedal ad lib. to end

WITH LOVE COMES A GREAT WATERFALL

By JOHN POWELL

THE HIDDEN WORLD

By JOHN POWELL

TOGETHER FROM AFAR

By JON THOR BIRGISSON

ONCE THERE WERE DRAGONS

By JOHN POWELL

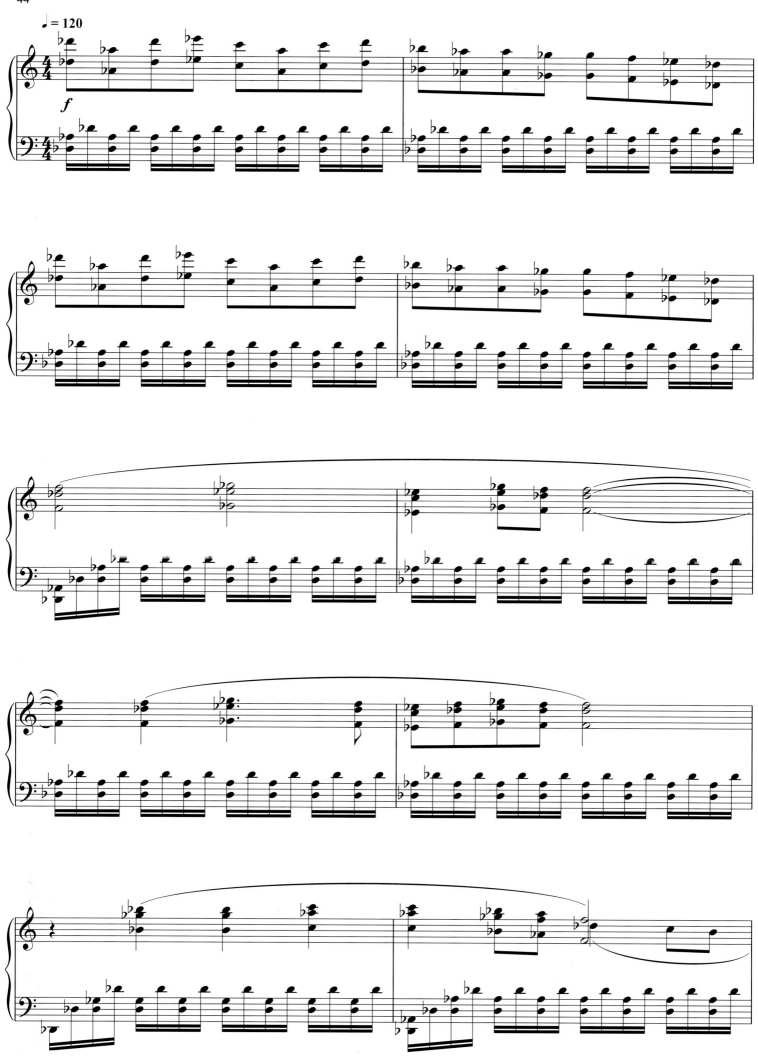